In the Belly
of the
Albatross

Patricia Caspers

GLASS LYRE PRESS

Cover art: "1025d" by Tia Marie McDermid
Design & layout: Steven Asmussen
Author Photo: Rick Caspers-Ross

Glass Lyre Press, LLC
P.O. Box 2693
Glenview, IL 60026

www.GlassLyrePress.com

CONTENTS

Oracle	9
Baby Catcher	10
Nana Ivy's Royal Typewriter	14
Hatsuhana Beneath the Waterfall	15
Gemini	17
What Mama Said	18
Mother & Child	19
La Fruta del Diablo	20
In the Belly of the Albatross	21
The Conservationist at Night	23
Whale Theory	24
Two Atheists on the Strait of Juan de Fuca	25
At Thousand Acre Swamp	26
Jobs for Which You May or May Not Have Been Paid	27
Hen's Bread	28
Rules for Living in the Belly	30
Aetos Kaukasios	31
Ekphrasis: 36 Ghosts, No. 5	32
Second Hand Bible	33
Bee Collector in Hospital	34
Of Some Things She Was Fond	35
Sculptor's Art (with Psalm 63)	36
I Loved a Republican	38
La Historia	39
The Book of Naomi	41
Five Stages of Grief	42
The Gorgon's Truth	45
No Sunrise	46
Unreported	47
Fledgling at Night	51
What I Am for You	52

Unearthed Notes of a Mother Welder   53

Daughter at 14, in Five Parts   54

Losing Your Daughter in the Bookstore   56

Mrs. Otis Earhart Awaits Her
         Daughter's Arrival, November 1937   57

winter, eleven   59

Vehicles   60

Irene's Goodbye   62

The Prison Guard's Wife   63

The Carousel Tender   64

Family Legend   66

The Squeeze Inn   67

Loss Prevention Specialist Blues   69

The Beekeeper's Widow   70

The Humming Dentist   72

The Learner   73

Since You've Been Away, the Garden   74

Letter to a Young Widow, with Geese   75

Astraphobia   76

What to Burn   77

Goodbye Is What Got Me Here   78

Piece by Piece   79

For Patricia Jean Caspers
(*1935-1984*)

ORACLE

Don't search for the answers, which could not be
given to you now, because you would not be able to
live them. And the point is, to live everything.
— Rainer Maria Rilke

What if an oracle lived at the end of your street
in a wonky red house with yellow trim,
a taffy-striped tabby named Kismet dozing on the stoop.

Would you wander through the snarl of wisteria
to take tea, bring a basket of August tomatoes
or a bucket of spring hydrangeas?
Would you court her prophecies?

In the kitchen, she reminds you of someone you used to know,
waving her arms fiercely to fill in the silence.
That's the way with oracles, you guess, thinking of Oedipus
and the details his priestess left out.

And what if this wise woman let it slip
that your brain's cogs will dull and seize one day:
Stairways will become as foreign to you as Istanbul,
where perhaps you would like to travel
while there's still time and equilibrium.

But now the crone must sleep.
She's already said too much, shooing
you through the front door. She clicks the bolt
and waves goodbye through the glass
while you stand in the bright evening,
mouthing the future.

BABY CATCHER

*If you hold your hand closed, nothing good can come
in. The open hand is blessed, for it gives in
abundance, even as it receives.*

— Bridget Mason

1.

I was born catching babies.
I caught spring lambs and calves in the fields
coming one after another so fast, no time
to wash the smell of God from my hands.

The white ladies in the big house screamed
foul-mouthed and scratched at the sheets
when I stretched the birth circle.
The babies pushed out blue and silent
or wailing pink. I passed 'em to their mamas and thought,
one day maybe you're gonna own me.

2.

I still sucked my thumb the day
they took me from my mama.
When you're tall as the corn, she said,
he's gonna come for you. Don't fight him.
I thought he'd sell me back to her.

The stickiest day of summer
when the house stunk sour with heat

10

he caught me up at the washtub.
I didn't cry out till, on my way home,
I saw the yellow stalks ready for harvest.

John Smithson put two girls inside me,
Ellen and Ann, and then he made
a wedding gift of me. When the groom
tore me open again, I got baby Harriet.

On Ellen's thirteenth, I gave her a knife.
God thinks it no sin, I said,
to kill the man stealing from you.

3.

African fever, autumnal fever,
canker rash, croup, king's evil, scrofula—
at ten I had touched 'em all
and hunted the woods for Jerusalem,
asafetida, snakeroot and boneset,
pounded and boiled 'em to medicine,
spooned the broth into waiting mouths.

4.

The icy mud swallowed my legs to the knees
as I pushed alongside the wagons—
Mississippi to Utah—
Baby Harriet on my back, while the girls
tugged at my skirts.

I tended the moaning cattle,
shoved and coaxed the sheep through rivers,
and caught impatient babies,
alive and steaming in the spring night.

By the time we saw that sky, wide as eternity,
and the buffalo, ugly as Judas and loud as God,
I'd wore my boot bottoms to skin.

5.

They hollered gold in California,
whispering freedom behind open hands,
and I was walking with the wagons again,
desert thirsty.

6.

That judge smelled like a fancy parlor,
and had eyes like January frost.
He almost spit red
when they called him abolitionist.
On court day he talked faster
than a spooked rabbit runs,
but he said freed woman,
and I didn't hear no more.

7.

Midwife, the doctor called me,
paid me $2.50 a day
to hold the hands of ailing white folks
in perfumed bed chambers,
and soothe their birthing daughters.
My people paid me in plucked chickens,
ripe tomatoes, snap peas, and kindness.
I kept my family's fill,
and gave Justice her dowry.

NANA IVY'S ROYAL TYPEWRITER

D-O-N . . . she pecked each key forcefully, the way her hen beaked the corn,

dabbed her forehead with a rose-scented kerchief.

"DON'T FENCE ME IN," she wrote,

returned to the kitchen, cranked the window handle,

let steam billow over the victory garden.

HATSUHANA BENEATH THE WATERFALL

I was a *wagyū* bride, sold
like prized beef, and wedding eve,
my groom took me
as he would one of the herd.

Katsugoro had a black-fisted
vengeance, and each *haru*,
when the stream chirped with frogs,
he sought his foe and left me
to wash the feet
of his oyster-eyed mother.

He would not return until
hatsuyuki, when angels
fell from the sky, seeking fire.
We had none to offer.

When Katsugoro snapped his legs
like dry bamboo, I wove him a cart
and trucked him high through the mountains
of windache to Tonosawa Falls.

Under the harsh wrath of water,
there was silence, and I prayed
for one hundred days.

Such a good wife, the villagers said.

Izanami-no-kami, I begged, you too
know a wife's grief. Please, wash this poison
from my breast.

On the hundredth day, she scrubbed my body clean
and swept me away.

GEMINI

Six weeks pregnant and you were scared of the mules.
Yet here was the oracle.
This was America's Delphi. You wanted a sign.
                              —Ted Hughes, "Grand Canyon"

I hike Havasupai with dirt-blistered feet.
Nauseous under the lamp of the moon and the balloon of my daughter
I pull myself by my own wrist
to where Havasu Falls lets loose its laughter.

I've learned that you once were here— what you were after,
and Sylvia, I think it's ironic
thirty years later I search this canyon—
my belly just as taut—
to baptize myself under the milk-water
of those falls.

Don't you know it's the water that breaks
over the dam and carries us home when we choose it?

WHAT MAMA SAID

I told Mama I gotta boulder in my belly.
She said that slag's gonna cost you
all your shiny pennies.

Mama heard the hummin' tune on my lips.
She said you better learn yourself a lullaby.

Mama, I said, I don't even cry no more.
That baby's gonna cry you a swimmin' hole, Mama said.
You float?

I told Mama I got dream wings.
She said you must be a ostrich, Girl.
You ain't flyin' nowhere.

MOTHER & CHILD

The baby startles with a hunger cry, and we wake again
in the blue milk light, angled through the blinds, illuminating
dust on forsaken surfaces. The refrigerator rumbles to stillness,
and the heater burns its morning-damp scent. The older children, cat,
husband all dream of alarm clocks while traffic is suspended, silent
during this cosseting hour when his cheek cups my breast, eyelids
flicker, and breath comes quick through a pressed nose.
We are the only two alive in the universe.
The nursling drinks, and there is only this
body-gift. We are of each other, wolfish, so animal,
I want to lick clean the crown-fur atop his moonbald head.

LA FRUTA DEL DIABLO

coyote makes no promises
anchor of sun
howl of rape trees
buitre, black as death's lashes
scorch blistered
mama's worry between my teeth
as a man might carry his knife
wind callused
mija, my light, *tres meses*,
buried beneath desert stones
no *identificado*
sleep soured
cross myself before the shadow river
la migra, la migra, la migra
Virgen de Guadalupe, to you I pray
before *la serpiente de la frontera*
swallows me, spits me
sin papeles
into fields of bloody fruit.

In the Belly of the Albatross

*A Hawaiian elder counseled us not to view the
albatross or the islands as victims of plastic pollution.
They have called this problem to them, she said, to
deliver us a message. We are hit with this message
every day. When can we say we're receiving it?*
—Victoria Sloan Jordan

Each of us is born into a cradle of loss

lamenting the briny absence,

pulse, echo, and mother-sway.

Each day we fill our bellies with lack:

umbilical ghost,

fallow breast,

silenced swaddling song

until we are anchored with nothings

as countless as a continent

of broken ocean bottles.

Our bodies swell with sorrow,

and the albatross heavies herself

on the bright remnants of our grief.

The Conservationist at Night

In the insomniac hours
she sometimes hears
the incantations
of seers and shamans,
and listens like a child
at her parents' bedroom door,
but their voices are shuttered
as if from the underside
of her pillow or through
the slow fog of another
universe where the spectacled
cormorant still dries its feathers
on unmined rocks
by a sea so clean
he can see through his own black
reflection to the passing
sweet eel— maybe
his afternoon catch—
all the way to the sand-
cradled bottom,
where he will dive, finally,
pulling her under.

WHALE THEORY

You thought their blue canticles
were meant for you, Love.

The chant of depths, the choral wail,
drawing your seaward return.

Oh, how you measured the wintering cadence,
slid the bracelet of each hour along your skin.

You smacked the sea with your broken boat,
dragged your sad instruments toward a quickening tenor.

Language, you named it: Grammar and Complexity.

Until, sprung under saltwater, you understood
the baleen heart, world enough alone

to hold you, your sloop full of algorithms,
and each one of your clangorous mistakes.

TWO ATHEISTS ON THE STRAIT OF JUAN DE FUCA

Mr. Tjemsland likes to check crab pots on Sunday morning
while Mrs. Tjemsland attends Mass, so that's what we do.

In his aluminum boat we skip the chop of wind and charcoal waves
toward orange buoys bobbing at us like old friends.

What he wrestles from the sea isn't a pot at all, but a wire circle, baited.
He explains the chicken neck, how a Dungeness scents it, crawls in,
       caught.

In the colder calm below the surface, he says, floats a maze of rusted
       cages,
abandoned by crabbers, their spoils forgotten.

Mr. Tjemsland's catch is full, though. Armored spiders
snap and pinch as he measures, flips their shells.

You gotta cook 'em in warm water, he says. *Too hot, they scream and run.*

I imagine Mrs. Tjemsland later, stoveside. As the crabs screech
and clamber for escape, she weeps into the gathering steam.

Mr. Tjemsland points the boat home. Beyond us Rainier sleeps,
its glaciers dulled by a smudge of rain.

AT THOUSAND ACRE SWAMP

Red Apple Farm, Phillipston, MA

There's a dead tree at the edge of the forest
where the apple trail narrows
and muddies itself out,
just before the geese announce themselves.

Must have been a conifer,
its trunk wider than any neighbor.
Now it's an armless torso
stretching skyward, the lower half
sculpted, carved, whittled, eaten,
raw heartwood exposed.

Each night the beavers leave the kits
to their own small gnawings, swim
from lodge to shore,
and begin again the slow felling
that began farther back than memory allows.

To passing hikers, this imminent toppling
seems a rodent's magnum opus, but maybe
the beaver has no grand ambitions,
just a moonlit yearning
to bite the work that needs chewing.

JOBS FOR WHICH YOU MAY OR MAY NOT HAVE BEEN PAID

Barista, Baby Sitter, Beggar of Bookstores,
Birthday Soprano, Candy Floss Fluffer,
Cake Maker, Creator of Goodbyes,
Cash Pocketer, Daughter,
Dishwasher, Egg Washer, File Girl,
Ice Cream Scooper, Ink Lasher, Liar,
Meringue Builder, Mother, Night Baker,
Parade Waver, Reader of Hopes,
Salad Girl, Secret Seeker, Seller of Wind Chimes,
Shoe Stacker, Spelt Packer, Tongue Biter,
Waitress in Sneakers, Wife, Wish Dasher,
Word Thief.

HEN'S BREAD

You didn't help me plant the wheat, water it, harvest it, or mill it and bake it, so I shall eat the bread all by myself.

— Little Red Hen

Red Hen sat at the flour-dusted
work table, her feathers
dough weary.

She inhaled the scent
of buttermilk and yeast,
sliced an end piece
from the still warm loaf,
smothered it with butter and honey,
but did not eat.

She heard the cuckoo's tick,
eyed the empty pine chairs.

Through her window
the afternoon went pink.

She watched Cat, Duck,
and Lazy Dog skip stones
across the pond,
nod their heads toward
each other.

She sighed, lifted the glass
and called to her friends,
Come eat this bread with me.

They widened their eyes at each other.
But we have no jam or tea to share,
cried the cat.

I know it, said Hen.
Your stories will do.

Rules for Living in the Belly

Make a brooch of your tongue,
a glittering gift of goodbye.

Keep your eyes. Grow them
into overripe oranges, but know
your light-starved pupils
will miss most everything.

Stretch your ears elephantine,
and hear the rattle of faraway rain,
the tap and scat of a ghostward father.

Memory is your scent now—
the bright spice of an Oregon cedar shop,
Grandfather's nicotine Ford, cologne of a gasolined shoe—
draw a fish hook in place of your nose.

There's no tunneling the mushroom dark,
but make a temple of your hands,
soak the callus ache each night
in honey cream, whisked egg, olive oil.

Let your nails go talon,
scratch each day's acrostic into the marl,
and when your body is funeral lichen
we may find your whittled rhymes, we may
read them.

AETOS KAUKASIOS

Hephaistos, that angry orphan God,
sculpted me of flame and metal,
bestowed upon me violent beak,
claws of nettle, and teased from me
the malice of nightmares.

He had no tenderness,
but offered instead a sunless sky,
fury's compass, and the chambered organ
of a stone-bound trickster.

Reader, I ate him.

Each day I returned to devour again
Prometheus's night-blooming liver.
It was not hunger that drew me,
but the pungency of his blood—
warm as lamp oil, sweet as compassion.

EKPHRASIS: 36 GHOSTS, No. 5

The stream was a collage of ice,
snow, fallen branches, hungry fish,
but her voice kept me warm,
whispered the ways she would
show thanks for the burden
of her willowed body upon my shoulders.

It was my old friend, Moon
and my wise rival, Water,
who uncovered her truth—
before we reached the pebbled shore—
her devil's tines, ogre teeth.

Quicker than lightning
I spilled her blood into the current,
and in its vermilion eddy
I saw the demon shine
behind my own eyes.

SECOND HAND BIBLE

This Bible is dust heavy, bought at a used bookstore,
the pages wrinkled and coffee circled.

I found her minister's letter here, between psalms.

He asks her to drink her tears by the bowlful,
and to have faith, as if faith is a long-nosed lapdog
that never yelps.

Did her hair shine then like broken egg shells ?
Did she wear silk dresses all shades of green
that twitched at her ankles?

Had she swallowed her heart for him,
the man who smelled of frankincense,
his accent as thick as his eyebrows?

And did he wrap her in his cassock under the willow tree at dusk,
leave her forever under the autumn blood moon?

I imagine her shrunken and silver now in a house that smells eternally
        of rain
and leaves on fire, smiling secretly sometimes while the rooster
outside her window crows and crows.

BEE COLLECTOR IN HOSPITAL

for dee ann

When they couldn't find her among the ceanothus, black sage, buckwheat, and poppies,
the bees swarmed the attic, into the bedroom sanctuary

where they sought her in the mesh of nets, glass jars, rows of tweezers and pins.
In furious confusion they tossed their velvet bodies against windows, each tap

a storm that gilded the draperies and bed clothes with a harvest of dust.
There was no one home to see it.

Each bee— bumble, honey, carpenter, and mason— lost its dance, held its cellophane
wings close, mumbled a song in sill corners until the heat, finally, took it.

She returned late, dazed and stitched, found her insect-loves brittle with sacrifice,
held them as tenderly as raindrops, inspecting each mandible, proboscis, and stinger.

She pinned them to the homasote, head to thorax, with the grace of a queen.

OF SOME THINGS SHE WAS FOND

Her hair, loosed from its elastic,
swing-brushing her freckled back.

Air bubbles leaping along her scalp
as she slid her body into the not-quite-scalding bath water.

Her belly's determined return
to its Willendorf contour.

Plucking the beastly whiskers from her chin
in the small, breath-fogged mirror.

A memory of an X-ray film in the doctor's hands, her bones
slight as a foal's legs.

The tongue-taste of dream essence collecting
on her upper lip in the night.

Dark cotton fluff tucked in the fold of skin
between her big nail and toe.

The occasional and exquisite
absence of pain.

Sculptor's Art (with Psalm 63)

> *Thus I can be yours, really yours, in getting more spirit from you, and in growing into a same spirit with you.*
>
> — Father Pierre Teilhard de Chardin to Lucile Swan

> *I can't have you. Not really, so I must learn your way of having each other.*
>
> — Swan to Fr. Teilhard de Chardin

With the clay warm in my hands I created the weather of your eyes.
My smallest finger dug the wrinkle of thought into your brow,

O God, thou art my God; early I will seek thee:
my soul thirsteth for thee, my flesh longeth for thee

so that I could see how you wanted, even after you left the sitting chair empty,
left the green of Peiping for the bones of the desert.

in a dry and thirsty land where no water is;
To see thy power and thy glory so as I have seen thee in the sanctuary.

I held your unfinished face in the heft of my palms, scored and slipped
the stubborn line of your nose and allowed for your breath.

Because thy lovingkindness is better than life, my lips shall praise thee.
Thus I will bless thee while I live: I will lift up my hands in thy name.

I carved and divided my heart, so that each half might be fettled
into the places where you listen to all of our unspoken words.

My soul shall be satisfied as with marrow and fatness;
and my mouth will praise thee with joyful lips:

You thought me as blind as Lucia, the winter saint for whom you said Mass
in the warmth of the basilica, while outside: virgin snowfall.

When I remember thee upon my bed, and meditate on thee in the night watches
Because thou hast been my help, therefore in the shadow of thy wings will I rejoice.

Remember I was the one who etched the wisdom of sunlight into your cheeks,
tapered gentleness into your lips and pressed God's secret, just there.

I Loved a Republican

once, and the heat of the imaginary flag
I threatened to burn suffocated
our long drive home.
He rolled his window low and shouted
me to prison, his words ricocheted
the windshield, smacked
almonds in the orchards as we passed.

With the flag we unfurled
into every fiery issue, and hoarse
in my parents' driveway, though it wasn't the end,
our goodbye was the slam of his Ford's weighty door.

Three administrations later, it's not
the photo of his startlingly blue-eyed wife
that stings me, the squishy infant in his arms,
or the gargantuan Oreo dane on his lead,

but the knowledge that his shepherd
and spaniel— following one another
nose to heel, sleeping in a close-tucked curl
beside the bed where we stole
our first naked afternoons—

are buried somewhere in a nearby field.

La Historia

So it was you then?
Mi querido, even then.

You worked dark mornings
until the fields of corn became sunlit,
and when your hands cracked and bloodied
you worked in those fields until you couldn't see
your blood on the corn.

I worked for Tía Zamora
in her dress shop in Matagalpa
cutting cloth from the bolt,
learning the selvage and the fold.
Seven days I worked, quitting only for Mass,
and in the evenings I walked five miles home to you.

We made sopa y tortillas
from bruised, stolen corn
and dreamed of California.
We were twenty-five then.

In 1906 Zelaya took the farms.
There was no work.
We spent all we had saved,
traveled by cargo boat
all the way to San Francisco.
My first time from home,
and I was sick with the salt,
the screeching gulls.

The city still burned when we arrived,
four days after the earthquake.

We walked through the tar-stink of fallen homes,
slept in the streets and ate apples
until we found a boarder home in Fruitvale
at the end of a beautiful, potholed road.

In this life
Fruitvale has no wildflowers,
only barred windows, stolen grocery carts.

We are twenty-five again.
You have lost your language,
and I am no longer de Nicaragua,
my skin as pale as moonlight,
but we are together in this overcast city,
where the smell of fresh corn
makes us homesick.

THE BOOK OF NAOMI

The Lord afflicts us all, my empty one,
so I will not be calling you Mara.
You are no more bitter than the barley
I glean for you each day.

You remember what I said
the last time you sent me away?
You saturate me the way blood-tea
stains the hot, clear water.

I never thought you'd anoint yourself sweet
and, yes, I've washed, worn my best clothes,
but I can't rinse your scent from my hair.

For all that you say, I will lie at his foot,
but I will dream of the moon-pale,
belly-soft, thigh-smooth of you,
the vinegar taste of your tongue, tied
to its root.

You can sell me as land,
trade sandals to close the deal,
and I'll go like good property,
but never again will you make me want
the salty grit of a man.

FIVE STAGES OF GRIEF

1. Denial

I want another language,
one that curves and rolls in the shape of her body.

She's everything with exception.

Her long fingers, May rain,
mouth, a red tulip blown open, black star centered.

Her tongue is a nervous cricket.
Her voice, a bracelet.

Pretty as a boy,
I like her best in her orange shirt on Fridays.

The day opens on us like a cracked egg,
the sun as fine as fuzz on a baby chick.

She's a bicycle without a chain.

I am an oak tree grown into its own barbed wire,
an origami note.

I am not that word
catching hard
at the back of her throat.

This is how to unhinge me.

2. Anger

<Silence>

3. Bargaining

If I could take back those fragile knives
spilling from my mouth,
swallow them again.

If I could whistle with two fingers.

It's a film that didn't match the sound,
the mouths moved,
but the words came too late.

A French movie in English translation
where language and smoke tumble from the mouth
of a cigaretted woman in black and white
but the subtitle reads only, "No."

Reverse the reel until the tape slaps
the projector.

Begin the language again.
Learn to conjugate.

If I could say, *écoute-moi*
would you?

4. Depression

Two women live in a blue craftsman
with a cut lawn and bloomed hydrangea,
diagonal from my apartment window.

Mornings I watch them warm the car
with its rainbow sticker across the bumper,
bundle their round-faced boy,
drive away together.

My breath clouds a knot on the glass.

5. Acceptance

Barefoot, I hunkered at that river,
studying flecks of pyrite.

I didn't know it would ache to stand,
that I would fight my own muscles.

And a voice can't be heard
over the sound of water rushing stone,
wresting it from the earth.

THE GORGON'S TRUTH

He called on me
in heat-hazy afternoons
as I dined on dust and apricots,

offered water from the sea
for my starlit bath,
praised the color
he brought to my cheeks, praised
my lashes as I turned away.

You think you know this story.

As a child my mother bade me
not to play with Gods,
so I accepted
Poseidon's gifts with a nod
and wished him *herete*.
Good day.
I had no use for any swain.

Some Gods will not be refused.

A new morning broke just the same.
Athena brought honey balm for my wounds,
washed the salt from my hair.

Give me the gift of monstrosity, I begged,
a face that mirrors the rage in my heart.
Let these locks gleam with the eyes of serpents.

No Sunrise

But a paling gray sky
bringing its own water
on November and the braided girl
who waited for the night train,
the men who offered a way home,
and the backroad tracks where they took her.

The rain dampened the girl's cries
as the men stole her only possession
with the same steel and flint
that sparked forth all of us.

We were each a pink and wrinkled seed
afloat in the saltwater grail, pressed
through the almond split,
crowding city hospitals,
flailing our arms
at the injustice of being born.

Even these men— created in a passion
alchemized to violence—
had mothers who believed
them into bloody life,
wet with womb water,
vernex thick in their tiny, blue creases.

Perhaps the undelivered signaled light
to that abandoned girl, like tarnished stars
flickering through the storm
from beyond the dark outskirts.

UNREPORTED

1.

The Girl I Was

wants to apologize
for the vodka sting
in her throat,
the giggling want
of the footballers
who tossed her like a pigskin,
her splash of laughter
under pool water,
piercing blue.

That girl lost
the soaked clothes
someone peeled away,
and she's sorry
for the replacements
two sizes too big,
with room enough
for the pug-faced one
to thrash
his freckled hands
past her waistband
and wrench open
the place where
she still smelled of chlorine.

And she didn't mean
for the room
to become a swirling

circus of rusted rings,
didn't intend to lose
her focus, to swallow
her voice, her breath,
as his friend took her—

she asks forgiveness
for not knowing where—

for waking up after,
bloody and sober,
stumbling alone
into a night
barren of stars.

2.

The Woman I Intend to Be

So many equinoxes later,
Persephone flings flip flops
and sunscreen into her satchel
at the first crack and mournful cry
of ice straining against the river's flow.
The ferryman paddles against the current,
and with each splash of the oar, each
knock of floe against the hull, the idea
of Hades blurs, as if it's a photograph
held so close the image dissolves, and soon
she's not even in the frame, and that night
in the meadow is gone. The hyacinth and crocus

become a dot-to-dot on the final page
in the book of her childhood. Like Sisyphus
she begins the mystery again,
but the 1 is never in the same place twice,
and the 2 is a freefall off the page,
into the next volume, Adulthood, a sequel
bereft of foreshadowing, whose narrator
is unreliable and easily sickened
by the scent of narcissus.

She plays dominatrix
to thin-boned, sweet-lipped
mortals who sigh that her body is a vessel,
her body is riverine. She fucks, and doesn't
return calls or read the poems
left on her doorstep. She fills her mouth
with wine, with almonds and olives,
and apricots, honey-steeped thiples, but nothing
washes clean the bitter seeds lodged
in her throat.

Who am I kidding?

I am no goddess. There is no spring
to beckon me from the underworld.
That boy has long since forgotten
my name. It's time
to dismantle this mausoleum of shame,
put down the "should haves," pick up the oars,
become the river, the craft, the orchard
of saplings in bloom on the far bank
where the slow spring light is indiscriminate,
and warmer now.

3.

The Mother I Am: An Open Letter to Demeter

Mother of Harvest, of Plenty, of Compromise,
These scales will never balance our horizon.
Time and again we've been patient
while men make gods and beasts of themselves,
gorge on our daughters, spit them into hell.
Listen, the judge has jizz on his hands.
His brothers devour Chicago dogs smeared with relish
and grunt approval from the sidelines.

The time for prayer has passed.

Gather the wronged: Persephone, Europa, Leda,
Medusa, Halpin, Washington, Havrilla,
the un-named in Stuebenville, in every country.

We will not pretty the ugly in them with
the shivs of our mouths. We may flinch
from the sucker punch of memory,
but we will not stop gathering the arsenal of our rage,
will not stop until we storm the fortress,
tear it down stone by stick, blaze the pyre,
and watch as every last fucker burns.

FLEDGLING AT NIGHT

As slow and sudden
as lengthening sunlight
she sleeps
while painted dolls hold vigil
and inside the shelter
of her body
a nest of fledglings
jostle and leap
or are nudged
by her mother-self,
and begin to fly,
fall, thudding
into that soft pasture,
where they wait to be washed
in the river current.
She wakes, and nothing
is changed, except
the vernal scent
only we trace
in the frozen air.

WHAT I AM FOR YOU

It's not like you work or anything
— Daughter, 14

candle lighter
spun weather vane
navigator of caprice
puddle spy
truth's gargoyle
surveyor of wounds
dog bellower
fry flinger
tomorrow's stalking lion
kitchen waltzer
commute queen
ambassador of kindness
soap spiller
mater pusher
untangler of knots
twister of tales
midnight's flashlight
czar of etiquette
sorry sloop
appointment illusionist
imagination's talisman
tear bower
fever swooper
sunbreak chanteuse
the silken thread tied
around Mnemosyne's wrist

Unearthed Notes of a Mother Welder

day 2,863:

my fingers no longer stretch
to catch the wind or curve to cup
fresh water to the fire of my mouth
but make a ladder, frozen
at the end of my torching arm

glove leather is fused to the fleshy seams of my palms
i've breathed the smoke of intention,
blinded myself with sparks of faith

and yet, the current is always too high,
the arc, too long, the weld cracks again

the metallurgist says it's impossible
to make art of a non-ferrous daughter,
a cast iron father, to sculpt them
into a composite family

i own i am heat weary,
but perhaps i'll try once more
with my heart as electrode
my blood, the flux

Daughter at 14, in Five Parts

1.

Reading

paperback and cake
kitchen table giggle girl
lost to this chored world

2.

Journaling

idea greedy
map, sketch, boy-puzzles, graph, chart
notebook universe

3.

Travel Weary

coast spliced and cry-eyed
she's lag-silent, goodbye full
flight stunned, all stillness

4.

Post Ride

high on the bascule,
she's palomino dreaming
so saddle savvy

5.

Overslept

bed flung and shrieking
she's a daybreak hurricane
as suddenly gone

LOSING YOUR DAUGHTER IN THE BOOKSTORE

You're in the scene from every mother's thicket-dark dream. You turn back
from the book of artists, and your daughter is not where you left her—
half in this world, cross-legged on a story hour carpet, half floating
in a mud pond with Frog and Toad— She's only a few steps away, you guess,
turn another corner, and another, until you're traversing the bookstore,
tightrope breathing, calling softly. You don't want to embarrass her. After
all, she's no longer the lost toddler in bus station nightmares that rush your
heart and wake you, dawn- startled. How long were you looking at that damn
Cassatt anyway? You cast a net of senses, become the espresso machine's
gasp, the sweet scent of magazine ink, a shiver of pages. You call louder, try
not to trod patrons as you hasten from aisle to rack, glance at the shamefaced
parking lot. Kidnapped. It happens. No time for her scream. You're about to
scream. You choke on a throatful of air, tilt your head back to bellow her name
and, oh, there she is: a blossom girl, grown into ripped skinny jeans, blonde
light behind Austen's paperback portrait, lingering sudden grace against the
banister, whispering Darcy's proposal to herself.

MRS. OTIS EARHART AWAITS HER DAUGHTER'S ARRIVAL, NOVEMBER 1937

I cannot leave the window. Wind. Oh.

Riveted here by a storm-addled kestrel spied beyond the glass,

her perfect architecture. *Fuselage.* God's streamline: she carries

even her breath on her back. And yet she's bested.

In her contraption, Millie shouted words of flight into the clouds

as if stitching the skies with precious stones, as if she'd become canary,
    uncaged:

Airfoils, Ailerons, Pitch, Propulsion, Thrust, & Yaw

I turn this lexicon on my tongue as one might worry the rosary.

It echoes hollow: bones of blackbird.

"Lady Icarus" folks whisper, but she knew better than that wax-winged
    fool, knew

the peril in a belly weighted by devotion.

And I suppose I should play Daedalus— cursed all the more

to an eternity of searching oceans for a single drowned feather.

But I wager she'll return

in a buzz of delight, with a wave of her wings and a chandelle flourish

or she won't return at all.

WINTER, ELEVEN

startle snow
blue-eyed ache and wonder
icicle child, lengthens and
vanishes into the hush

yesterday's rain fairy,
tomorrow's sleet soldier,
3 o'clock hunger and hustle

born a mouthful of worry,
she dreams the frozen lake
into flux and thaw

wades past the blue dark,
under the leafy muck—
feels her blood slow, her heart
imperceptible

she frog-sleeps, her limbs
numb and water heavy
as the ice closes over, shelters.

a woman in hard light,
scents out the season,
knows— come spring—
her girl will swim.

VEHICLES

The year they created
the mobile home
Grandma was born
and grew up summers
at the ocean,
making tuna fish sandwiches.

My mother came crashing
into the world
two months before James Dean
sped his Spyder
through the intersection
into a common Ford.

The Lunar Rover drove through
moon dust while
my father's sperm traveled
my mother's fallopian tubes
collided with an egg
in the back seat of a Dodge Dart
in a parking lot
on a Saturday night.

Now
Grandma's gotta Fat Boy.
She swings her leg over the machine
lifts the stand
turns the key
jumps the kick start
squeezes the clutch,
revs it up
her left foot clicks it into first,

and she brumbles out of the trailer park.
Takin' it up for some Oregon rain.

IRENE'S GOODBYE

Listen here,
don't matter if the sun shinin' itself
all over the place outside—
we got rain in this rabbit warren
every goddamn day.
Nurse tells me I gotta take three blue pills
on Tuesday, two white pills on Friday,
and one pink pill every in-between day,
and if I do, I get myself some nice vanilla
ice cream after supper— she thinks
I'm some pansyfaced girl with pigtails
gotta learn to mind her manners—
but I don't want no more how-dee-do
ice cream. I had me five lifetimes
before that pajama-bottom nurse
quit her mama's milk, and now
I wanna cozy down in the deep pocket
of some small town lounge,
draw on a freshly lit Parliament
and palm myself a glass full of fire
while the pool balls smackthud
and a clean-shaven man with motor oil cologne
cracks a joke, slides in close,
and sambas his fingers across my thigh.

Hell if I ain't gonna roll me there.

THE PRISON GUARD'S WIFE

Hyrtle, your great-papa, was a guard out at Folsom.
We lived in a house near the prison gate.
I could see the boys working in chains
through my kitchen window.
They weren't like those criminals today.
If I needed a single thing — firewood chopped —
the guard let 'em come down and help.
I never was afraid for the babies.
Those men were sweet like
the blackberry pie and coffee I'd give 'em.
They were thankful.
Taking cheese sandwiches to Hyrtle,
I walked right on by 'em,
all so dear-lord dirty in their work clothes.
They winked at me when I passed.

THE CAROUSEL TENDER

The dead always choose
the milk-painted ponies,
made of basswood and poplar
with tails of fine Tersk.

And the dead never bother
with paper tickets
softened by weather.

They shrug one shoulder,
and give her a wink long since
put by for sweethearts and beaus.

This is how she knows them.

The Wurlitzer wheezes,
"Come Josephine in My Flying Machine,"
and the carousel tender
climbs into the operator box
where she shuts out the sound
of the bally talker's call,
the smell of fresh kettle corn,
and the queue of eager children
jostling the velvet rope.

Her grandmother came to ride once
in her cotton dressing gown,
bare feet damp with sand.
She smelled of the sea and salt
water taffy, and chose the sun-
faded prancer with glass black eyes.

The platform rattled around,
the cranking rods twirled,
and the dapple grey galloped her,
sidesaddle and laughing,
'til the organ tired itself out.

"Take me with you," the tender cried,
as her grandmother blew a kiss goodbye,
and scattered like ashes over the bay
on a windy autumn evening.

FAMILY LEGEND

No one was there the morning you answered
the rotary phone at the end of the hall.
No one heard what you said to the polite-
voiced woman who called you by your birth
name— a name she found in the book—
perhaps you thought it was a sales call,
or a creditor, a distant aunt
pleading for money.

And then she said your husband's name,
the name of my grandfather, who was then
still tough as alder, and that tall.

How did you find her? I imagine
a raven-haired woman, like your mother,
smoking lipstick-stained cigarettes
on your sofa, legs crossed.

Legend goes, the pair of you scarved your heads
and drove the convertible— I like to think
it was yellow— past the yard where Papa
stacked soda cans onto trucks. That's where
he saw you with your Miss America smiles
and royal waves.

At 5 o'clock, calm in your rage,
you promised your dog-faced husband
three things: You would one day counter his betrayal.
He would never know when, and he would never
speak of it.

THE SQUEEZE INN

The last time I tied this blue bandana
around my head was the night
I looked up from the fridge
where I was scrubbing the veggie drawer,
and your father was leaning
against the doorway, as if
he belonged there,
as if it hadn't been a year or more
since the bracelet slipped
from his fling's wrist
onto my pillow.

You didn't have to get all
gussied up for me, he said,
and I smacked him between
those blue eyes with a rubber glove.

My new honey had a date with Jack Daniels
at the Weepin' Willow. We'd be
married within the month.

Your father drove me to a quarter box motel,
next highway over,
and we had ourselves a time —
like we were inventing something.

I slept an hour, dreamed I
was a climbing rose. Petal poor,
I bloomed thorns.

I woke to the stink of Marlboros
sifting the walls of another room

and your father's familiar
night noises.

I watched him sleep and realized,
all our knotted, married nights
this is where he lay, another woman
awake in his warmth, wondering
at the gold band on his wedding finger.

I'd never left a room so silently.

LOSS PREVENTION SPECIALIST BLUES

All day I watch pixelated women
on a black and white monitor
in a soundless, windowless room,
and though the dresses they slip on
or squeeze over their bodies
are gray on my screen, I know
the peach, vermilion, lilac of each, and how many
days work it would cost,
how many dinners uneaten, how many
miles walked for saved bus fare.
They suck their bellies, fidget
their breasts, and I imagine
the way your eyes would go wide,
when you opened your door,
and found me in the blue sheath,
how we'd drive all night
with the windows low,
until we reached a lean stretch of beach, and then
we'd play the radio, doors wide as wings,
and sand dance real slow
until the sun glinted the ocean,
the car, the beak of a seagull in search
of one uncracked oyster.

THE BEEKEEPER'S WIDOW

In the welting wind my love
rasped the waxed frames clean,
and from his cold, gloved hands
offered candling pearls:
wing-paned, chocolate dark,
a linden scent.

One spring midnight, our bed empty,
I found him hive-sleeping,
his shorn hair moon lit, static heavy.
I spied until the sun drew a golden thread
across the mountains,
watched him rise with the grist,
dawn-dancing.

All that season he was a swirl of apple blossoms.
I tried to catch the petals like snowflakes on my tongue.

When the leaves were unfolding origami
he breathed a feral wine,
smudged the house with pear cinders,
ever-humming hosannas in his sleep.

Anniversary eve, I bathed myself
in clover water, cottoned my body
with honey perfume,
waited beneath the bridal quilt.

But I was too late. Queen charmed,
he battered at locked windows,
the force of his desperation
a twilight tapping that reflected

small, blue sparks in the glass.

Morning-grieved, I heard
the distant call of a queedling shrike,
flung the windows wide,
and tore down the screens.

THE HUMMING DENTIST

She likes mouths, the many shades
of pink Os opening
and closing— chapped or glossed.
The smell of sweet numbing alcohol,
and the gentle injection.
The vibration of the drill in her hand.
The tongue, that slippery muscle
hiding in the cheek,
or wrestling with her instrument.
She likes the pine nuts of our teeth
carved and patched
into miniature monuments
of herself.

THE LEARNER

The kitchen sweats against us,
and it's not Mexico
but warm California valley orchards
where I teach him *I want more*
in hard flat American English,
concentrate on the waves
of his rolling Rs.
He touches my hair, winter brown,
wishes it gold again.
He draws a thin line
along the scar on my forehead.
I learn, *no tengo nada*
in soft double negatives.
And his wife all the time
his wife
escuchando
scrubs potatoes clean
under cold running water.

SINCE YOU'VE BEEN AWAY, THE GARDEN

is drought stricken

and tongues of bean vine
strangle the corn in its husk.

Zucchini shade bests slender
stems of pepper stalks.

Summer squash curls
reptile-skinned
beneath a wilted green skirt
sequined in Brandywines.

Katydids jeer
from sunflower heights.

Did you never receive my letter?

Evenings I fling

copper-barreled beetles from chewed leaves
into a bowl of soapy froth

until nightfall declares one of us
the victor.

Come home before the frost
and we'll bury the hyacinth bulbs.

LETTER TO A YOUNG WIDOW, WITH GEESE

All black-necked pluck
and brown feather quiver,
the Canada goose has no obligations.

We expect a goose to plan, to migrate—
flap and wing rush to Mexico—
but there is nothing a goose must do.

He may remain, like grief,
in the marsh pond of your belly,
in the golf course of your heart.

Labradors can't bark him away.
Shotguns don't deter him.

He lives heavy where a home is made,
intended or not, here in California, and there
in your funereal summer.

You may have spied him
in the croplands that day,
your car window rolled low,
the wind doing what the wind does,

just before.

ASTRAPHOBIA

When in the night's lean hours
lightning blazes your window,
and thunder gives it
a standing ovation,
when your dog paws her way
into your still motion dreams,
take the day's heavy simmer
to the unswept linoleum,
scratchy wool rug,
or cool, coiled, pine.
Don't ask for sleep,
but hold her dark,
furred body as you would
a nightmared child,
grieving lover,
breathe her river scent,
rest in thankfulness
for one creature who still needs
every broken piece of you.

What to Burn

The tender heart of softwood
lights with fury, fills the house
with a feral scent that reminds you
of solstice twilights,
but fir and pine
are bested by the ache
of a February midnight.
You will find in your hearth
only morning's lone wolf.

A faithful husband
who never swelters,
madrone's slow burn
holds you dear through daybreak.
Whim will be your tithing.

When the stove is a black yowl
build a pyre of tarot cards,
kindle fallen birch, burn the matches.

When the fire at last gorges
every empty journal,
make of your body
a palimpsest.

Bathe in the ink flood
of your chattering hands.

GOODBYE IS WHAT GOT ME HERE

Khoda hafaz is one way to leave
a family, the broken skeleton key of home,

the constellations of star thistle
singing *zai jian* along thirsty hillsides.

Moog zoo is the goodbye of rice paddy roads
low slung and sun-bleached between greenwater fields.

California's *paalam* is a feral mustang
rearing in protest of lost currency,

a papier-mâché boomerang, its newspaper *do vstrechi*
more tattered upon each return.

There's one way to say *bedkee yertam hima*
to one who waves through the empty space

of a Chevy's lowered window,
another— *annyong-hi kyeshipshio*— for one

who's left behind, whose distant farewell is swallowed
by the branches of a sidewalk sycamore.

I am both.

PIECE BY PIECE

1.   Construction

When the road was not a road but a flooded mouth of broken teeth
husband and wife parked at the spring-swollen dam.

Above a chorus of peepers they bickered the radio news
unloading their haul: soft pine, tongue, groove.

They shouldered the wood under a catchpenny moon.
A quarter mile down they filled the waiting cabin.

He laddered himself against the morning dark,
hammered walls, the plums of his thumbs, oiled knots,

while she cupped nails in her slivered hands.
Just like playing house, she thought.

2.   Renovation

Groom, bride, cloven claw of crow bar, caliper
of mood, chest of contraption between them.

In each dark pine coil she sees flow
of grain obstructed, accuser's warped eye, rosined wound.

Not optic, he says, planetary; solar system
multiplied, universe contained.

Become a frisky god, she says, and swings her iron tool.
Tear apart the cosmos. Let there be a new kind of light.

END NOTES

"Baby Catcher": Based on the biography of Bridget Mason, freed slave and one of the first Black women to own land in Los Angeles, California.

"Hatsuhana Beneath the Waterfall": A re-telling of the Japanese legend, based on the woodblock print, *Hatsuhana Prays Under a Waterfall*. Wagyū: Beef; Haru: Spring; Hatsuyuki: First snow of the season; Izanami-no-kami: Japanese Goddess of birth and death.

"La Fruta del Diablo": The devil's fruit; Buitre: Vulture; Mija: My daughter (endearment); Tres meses: Three months; Identificado: Identification; La migra: Border Patrol; Virgen de Guadalupe: Our Lady of Guadalupe; La serpiente de la frontera: The border snake; Sin papeles: Without papers (undocumented).

"Ekphrasis: 36 Ghosts, No. 5": A re-telling of the Japanese legend and print, *Omori Notices a Demon*.

"Sculptor's Art": Based on the relationship and letters of Father Pierre Teilhard de Chardin and Lucile Swan.

"Aetos Kaukasios": Based on the Greek myth of the eagle that fed upon the re-generating liver of Prometheus.

"The Learner": No tengo nada: I have nothing; Escuchando: Listening.

ACKNOWLEDGMENTS

I'd like to thank the editors of the following publications where these poems were first published, possibly as earlier drafts or with different titles: "Bee Collector in Hospital," *Adirondack Review*; "Conservationist at Night," *Anderbo*; "Oracle," *Chest Magazine*; "Family Legend," "Whale Theory, " *Barrier Islands*; "Two Atheists on the Strait of Juan de Fuca," *Cortland Review*; "The Gorgon's Truth," *Fjord's Review*; "Hatsuhana Beneath the Waterfall," *Futurecycle Press*; "Mother & Child," *Generations*; "La Historia," *Nimrod*; "Baby Catcher," *PANK*; "Piece by Piece," *Ploughshares*; "Letter to a Young Widow, with Geese," "Losing Your Daughter in the Bookstore," "Mother & Child," "Unearthed Notes of a Mother Welder," *Quiddity*; "Unreported," *R.K.V.R.Y*; "The Prison Guard's Wife," *Rose and Thorn*; "Gemini," *Spillway*; "Mrs. Otis Earhart Awaits Her Daughter's Arrival, November 1937," "The Beekeeper's Widow," *Superstition Review*.

First I would like to thank Glass Lyre Press for its big yes, as well as my patient professors at Chico State University and Mills College for their time and attention: Carole Simmons Oles, Gary Thompson, Elmaz Abinader, Chana Bloch, and Elizabeth Willis. I'm grateful to the fine folks at Hedgebrook who supported me with solitude, delicious meals, as well as the gift of lasting friendships. I am so thankful to my writing group of twelve years: Katherine Case, Annie Stenzel, and Jennifer K. Sweeney, for their keen eyes, gentle critique, and deep love of cheese and chocolate. To Lisa Ahn and Laura Hall Grodrian, poets in novelist's clothing, I'm also thankful for word wisdom and insight. Finally, thank you to my mom, Sandy Floyd, for supporting me, and to my husband, Rick Caspers Ross, for always seeing me.

About the Author

Patricia Caspers is the founding editor of *West Trestle Review* and poetry editor for *Prick of the Spindle*. She lives with her family in Auburn, California.

Glass Lyre Press

exceptional works to replenish the spirit

Glass Lyre Press is an independent literary publisher interested in technically accomplished, stylistically distinct, and original work. Glass Lyre seeks diverse writers that possess a dynamic aesthetic, and an ability to emotionally and intellectually engage a wide audience of readers.

Glass Lyre's vision is to connect the world through language and art. We hope to expand the scope of poetry and short fiction for the general reader through exceptionally well-written books, which evoke emotion, provide insight, and resonate with the human spirit.

Poetry Collections
Poetry Chapbooks
Select Short & Flash Fiction
Anthologies

www.GlassLyrePress.com

CPSIA information can be obtained
at www.ICGtesting.com
Printed in the USA
FSOW01n1128180416
19348FS